Hope from the Margins

New Ways of Being Church

Lecturer in Evangelism, Spurgeon's College, London

Anne Wilkinson-Hayes

Minister, South Oxford Baptist Church

GROVE BOOKS LIMITED
RIDLEY HALL RD CAMBRIDGE CB3 9HU

Contents

The Cover Illustration is by Peter Ashton

Church Army and the Grove Evangelism Series

Church Army has over 350 evangelists working in five areas of focus, at the cutting edge of evangelism in the UK. It co-sponsors the publication of the Grove Evangelism Series as part of its aim of stimulating discussion about evangelism strategies, and sharing its experience of front-line evangelism.

Further details about Church Army are available from:
Church Army, Independents Road, Blackheath, London SE3 9LG.
Telephone: 0181 318 1226. Fax: 0181 318 5258.
Registered charity number: 226226

First Impression February 2000
ISSN 1367-0840
ISBN 1 85174 425 8

1
Introduction

Now that the Decade of Evangelism has ended and a new century has dawned, it is time to take stock. We offer here a brief analysis of the impact of this decade and of the current state of the churches. Our conclusions are that, despite some encouraging signs, the church is in trouble and that discovering new ways of being church is a crucial task in the coming years. We then tell stories of experiments, communities and initiatives that may provide clues for our continuing search for such new ways. These are not success stories but diverse expressions of church on the margins. We believe that in a post-Christendom context the church will need to learn once again to operate from the margins, so we have chosen to examine marginal expressions of church life for signs of hope. We have identified some of the questions raised by the stories and have begun the process of engaging in theological reflection on these. We invite readers to share their own experiences of new ways of being church, to search out other models and to continue this process of reflection. Is there really hope from the margins?

2
A Church in Crisis?

The Church in a Time of Change

Many words beginning with 'post-' featured in Christian writings in the 1990s: post-evangelical, post-charismatic, post-liberal, post-denominational, post-Christendom—to name but a few. Similar words are evident throughout contemporary culture: post-ideological, post-structural, post-feminist, post-industrial, post-secular, post-colonial, and, most popular of all, post-modern. Sometimes dismissed as trendy, this terminology at least indicates a significant mood within our culture.

Often the meaning of the term is unclear. 'Post-' (literally 'after') denotes change rather than indicating much about any future direction. We live in an era of flux, where past certainties are being questioned, past structures overturned and past answers re-examined. There is no way yet to know how much will survive from what has been familiar, what new features will gain acceptance, or how these will be blended together in an increasingly diverse culture. There are

3

more questions than answers at present.

For the church this is a time of both challenge and opportunity, an unsettling time and a time to reflect in fresh ways on what it means to be church and what the mission of this church is. As in other parts of society, so in the church it may well be that we have more questions than answers as yet, but at least there is a new freedom to ask questions, experiment and engage in reflection.

And there is evidence of reflection and experimentation. Books and articles on new ways of being church have appeared. Networks of people devoted to exploring new models of church have held consultations. And several new kinds of church life have emerged: seeker services; youth churches; ethnic churches; cell churches; base churches; cyber-church; and a renewed interest in communities. Some of these may be distractions or dead-ends. Others may hold vital clues for the future.

Reflecting on the 1990s

Recent emphasis on church planting may also indicate an openness to new ways of being church. Stuart Christine suggests: 'Creative church planting that discovers new ways of being the Body of Christ in a changing world will help keep the sinews of our denominations supple and more able to respond sensitively and vigorously to the as yet unforeseen challenges of tomorrow's world ...New churches, and the fresh theological insights that they generate, counter the tendency to ecclesiological ossification that turns structures into strictures.'[1]

However, church planting, which was advocated strongly during the 1990s, has not accomplished as much as its advocates were hoping for; nor have the evangelistic initiatives of the Decade of Evangelism. Unrealistic goals set early in the decade have not been reached, church membership has continued to decline, and fewer churches have been planted as the decade has progressed. The decline in church planting is due to a number of factors:[2]

- most churches which were able to plant another church early in the 1990s have not yet recovered sufficiently to do so again;
- few newly planted churches have yet grown quickly enough to plant another church;
- the dominance of personnel-intensive models of church planting have discouraged smaller churches from becoming involved;
- a disturbing number of church plants have failed, have remained small and weak, or have attracted only those who were already Christians;
- church planting has generally been restricted to areas where churches are

1 Martin Robinson and Stuart Christine, *Planting Tomorrow's Churches Today* (Tring: Lion, 1995) p 54.
2 These factors are not well documented but are familiar to consultants and practitioners. Some were already apparent earlier in the decade, as is evident from Derek Allen's report into Baptist church planting, *Planted to Grow* (Didcot: Baptist Union, 1994).

already flourishing, leaving many urban and rural areas untouched;
- limited resources have hindered the development of a national church planting initiative;
- parochial boundaries have inhibited church planting in Anglican circles;[3]
- other initiatives (especially *Alpha* and cell churches) have taken centre stage during the second half of the decade;
- yearnings for revival and short-term millennium projects have hindered strategic mission planning.

It is too early to assess any lasting impact of this decade on church and society in Britain. It has not increased the overall number of churches or church members, but it may have been a catalyst for fresh thinking about evangelism and church life.[4] Several features of the changed landscape are already apparent:
- important shifts in thinking about evangelism have taken place—from large-scale to local, from technique to friendship, from monologue to dialogue, from proclamation to demonstration, from crisis to process;[5]
- church planting is now endorsed by many denominations as a vital component within their national mission strategy;
- the concept of missionary congregations has become familiar and congregations are exploring the implications of moving from maintenance towards the mission stance required in a post-Christendom context;
- the proliferation of new models of church indicates dissatisfaction with familiar models of church (including the so-called 'new churches,' which have not sustained their rapid growth of the 1980s and early 1990s);
- the suspicion is growing that enlarging existing churches through more effective evangelism is not enough, and that reproducing existing models of church through church planting will not do.

A Church in Trouble?

So where does this leave us at the start of a new millennium? It is possible that the first decade of this new century will witness an upsurge in church planting. It may be that a more contextual approach to evangelism will begin to bear fruit. But it seems clear that, despite all that has been attempted and accomplished in the past ten years, the church in Britain is in trouble—even crisis. Despite exciting but sporadic signs of growth (such as the proliferation of ethnic churches in London and elsewhere), some creative initiatives and much talk of revival, the church has continued to decline and age, and it shows no sign of imminent recovery. Most denominations are struggling; some appear to be in

---

3 On this issue, see David Pytches and Brian Skinner, *New Wineskins* (Guildford: Eagle, 1991) and Nigel Scotland (ed), *Recovering the Ground* (Chorleywood: Kingdom Power Trust, 1995).
4 On this see further Robert Warren, *Signs of Life* (London: Church House, 1996) and *Setting the Agenda: Lessons from the Decade of Evangelism* (London: Church House Publishing, 1999).
5 On these and other shifts, see two books by John Finney, *Finding Faith Today* (Swindon: BFBS, 1992) and *Recovering the Past* (London: Darton, Longman & Todd, 1996).

meltdown. Many more churches will close within the next two decades.

Not only is there numerical decline, but many churches, including some presently large and growing congregations, are increasingly distant from contemporary culture. Spirituality—in diverse shapes and forms—is back in vogue; but most churches are struggling to connect with this. The complaint from within youth culture is no longer that the church is boring but that it is not spiritual enough! Nor often does it seem greatly concerned about social justice and the flourishing of human communities. The gulf between the 'haves' and the 'have nots' in our society continues to widen; but the church is unsure how to break out of its suburban and provincial captivity. There are wonderful exceptions, of course, but too many are simply not engaging with contemporary culture or social issues. Unsurprisingly, the prevailing attitude towards church is not hostility but indifference.

Furthermore, many churches are failing to provide even their own members with a meaningful experience of community, opportunities to encounter God or resources for daily discipleship. Multiple and predictable meetings with ecclesiocentric preaching exhaust the faithful but do little to equip Christians to live out their faith in a changing society. Large numbers of our most committed members are leaving our churches, including many leaders. Why? Irrelevance, fear of 'the world,' ghetto-mentality, introversion, narrow-mindedness, over-commitment, judgmental attitudes, boredom, inflexibility, fundamentalism, clerical dominance, sexism, racism, the confusion of gospel and culture, reductionist approaches to mission, imperialistic and patronizing attitudes towards others, absorption with trivial issues and many other reasons are given. In 1992, Morris Stuart wrote passionately about the exodus from the churches of committed, gifted and now deeply disillusioned Christians. His book, *So Long, Farewell and Thanks for the Church?*[6] contains several letters written by 'refugees' from the churches, which make painful but illuminating reading. In 1995, David Tomlinson wrote *The Post-Evangelical*[7] drawing on his own discontent with much contemporary church life and on conversations with others who had left their churches.

What follows is set against this background of a changing culture and a church in a time of transition—perhaps of crisis. Our aim is modest. We do not attempt to address the major missiological and ecclesiological issues facing the church in Britain today. We simply offer stories of new ways of being church which have emerged in recent years, together with brief reflections on what these might signify. We have chosen these examples, not because of their size, rapid growth, dynamic leadership or impressive organization, but because they pose important questions. Some of them have been deliberately planted. Some have devel-

---

6 Morris Stuart, *So Long, Farewell and Thanks for the Church?* (Milton Keynes: SU, 1992).

7 David Tomlinson, *The Post-Evangelical* (London: Triangle, 1995). Although this book relates mainly to evangelical charismatic church life—the sector most involved in evangelism and church planting—many of its concerns have a wider application.

oped through the renewal of existing churches. Some have emerged accidentally. They are diverse, tentative and marginal, but also provocative.

We wonder whether these stories may help us explore issues that many churches will face in the coming years. We present them here, not as success stories, but as question marks, as clues, as possible signs of hope.

3

Signs of Hope?

What is Church?

How we define church obviously affects the examples we select as hopeful. Different individuals and groups will have their own definitions and criteria for hopefulness. As we introduce the following examples and reflect on why they seem hopeful to us, we should identify our own perspectives. Our definition of 'what is church?' and our framework for reflection are undoubtedly shaped by our Baptist and Anabaptist backgrounds and convictions.

However, we would claim also that our determining factors arise from some key characteristics of the early churches, the communities closest to the teaching and life of Jesus. The church grew in the first four centuries at a far more rapid rate than in subsequent generations, and research has highlighted several significant elements to this growth. These include a real sense of Christian community, a willingness to serve the society around, and a distinctive lifestyle, which intrigued and fascinated people.[8] It is these three factors which we look for in our 'signs of hope.'

The following examples include unintentional churches, church plants, resurrected churches, groups that would class themselves as Christian communities rather than churches, and some that would not call themselves church at all!

The Hope Community

Three Roman Catholic religious sisters were asked by their parish church to conduct a community survey in Heath Town, Wolverhampton—a nine tower-block estate with much social need. The sisters went into the estate every day and simply listened to people's pain and despair. As time went by, they felt increasingly ill at ease returning to their own house in a comfortable suburb and

---

8   See further Alan Kreider, *Worship and Evangelism in Pre-Christendom* (Joint Liturgical Studies 32, Cambridge: Grove Books, 1995).

so rented a maisonette on the third floor of one of the tower blocks. They continued their life of community and prayer from this flat, and were available to local people. Their presence catalysed many social changes, although they did not set out to initiate anything. Estate services have begun—planned and led by local people. Computer courses have started, holidays, celebrations, literacy training have all improved the quality of life. Their strength of community has been central to this way of being church. Their small community has helped create greater community in the wider and otherwise dysfunctional setting.

The sisters would not publicly call what happens 'church,' but members of the local community perceive the third floor maisonette as the chapel for the estate. Sister Margaret Walsh tells the lovely story of a local man in prison, asking to phone his Mother Superior![9] A key theological reflection on this way of doing church is that the sisters resisted any notion of imposing anything. Their aim throughout has been to discover what God was already doing in people. There is no idea of taking God to people—they see that as part of the power relationship that many people at the bottom of the heap resent. Rather, their focus is to enable people to see God in the everyday.

Living Proof

This emerged on the outskirts of Cardiff out of a house group, who were a little disillusioned with church life and wanted to be more relevant in how they lived out the gospel. 'There must be something more!' was their cry. They spent time praying and came to the unlikely conclusion, given they had no children of their own, that it was to be work with local children.[10]

They started a small Bible club in 1984. This was initially very traditional church-based Christian youth work, but it grew over the years until they were running clubs six days a week, for all age groups. Following a visit to New Jersey in 1993, Living Proof was born—an approach to youth work which involves teaching life skills to young people through teaching them to care for younger young people. In several local schools the courses are now a fully accredited part of the curriculum. Their summer play schemes are very popular—involving 1500 children over the five weeks and drawing on the skills of dozens of volunteers. The Living Proof catch-phrase is that 'everybody is special'; all their courses are imbued with this ethos. It makes a huge difference to many very disenfranchised children and is valued by authorities and parents.

So far, Living Proof was just a good example of Christian community work, but the children began to see staff meeting for prayer and asked to join them. Young people became Christians on Living Proof weeks, but where could they go for discipleship? They did not fit into local churches. Soon there were too

---

9 Margaret Walsh, *Here's Hoping! Urban Theology Unit New City Special No 8* (1991).
10 The Living Proof story is told by George Lings, in the series of booklets *Encounters on the Edge*, available from the Sheffield Centre, 50 Cavendish Street, Sheffield S3 7RZ.

many to fit in a house and they started meeting in a community centre. It was never their intention, but they discovered they had a church. The young people themselves have developed a different approach. They have discussion, prayer and worship on Sunday evenings, but on Sunday morning they have 'Sunday service'—activities like singing in Old People's homes, cleaning graffiti, helping in Sunday schools of smaller churches.

Now the leaders are ordained and Living Proof is recognized as an Anglican church plant, with an inter-denominational congregation. It will be interesting to see if the label changes the fresh and imaginative approach they have developed. This story suggests that, when kingdom work happens in a way that truly engages the whole person, church in an authentic form emerges.

The Furnival

George MacCleod speaks of Iona as a thin place where heaven and earth come very close. Our brief encounters with The Furnival in Sheffield had been similar, but any visit is merely a snapshot in time, and a concern in telling these stories is that exposure can sometimes damage fragile experiments.

The Furnival, which has been recently publicised through a Baptist Union Home Mission video,[11] is an example of resurrected church. The last formal Christian witness on the notorious Burngreave Estate ended when the Methodist Church closed, but four elderly members refused to believe God had given up on the estate and continued to meet and pray in each other's homes. They were right. Jane Grinnoneau experienced an extraordinary call to minister in the derelict pub on the estate when she was lost on her way to the Urban Theology Unit. Her story of the miracles of acquiring the building and fitting it out to meet local needs is very special. From vandalised, stripped pub it has become a skills centre for young people, a training kitchen and café, and surrounding buildings have been earmarked for a launderette and multi-agency health and advice centre. As Josie's story on the video illustrates, local people are being touched by the love and grace of Christ.

The Furnival would resist being labelled a church plant, as this puts the focus on the wrong area. They say church, as we currently use the term, is too closely identified with congregational meetings for worship. Worship and prayer are the fuel and lifeblood of their activity, but the work is discovering the kingdom of God among local people. Church at The Furnival is about being the yeast that ferments change in the dough. They do not invite people to 'come to church' but to find God's love and acceptance as they work for wholeness in the community through various projects and initiatives. Everything done in Christ's name, or wherever love is revealed, is church in the true sense. The word 'church' is used less and less as it creates more barriers than it overcomes.

---

11 Available from BU Publications, Baptist House, Didcot, OX11 8RT.

The Crowded House

A different Sheffield-based group meets in a substantial Victorian house. Emerging as an offshoot of a large Anglican church, the group have developed a pattern of life, service and worship unencumbered by any building. When challenged about how people find out about them, they explain that they serve their 'virtual community'—that is, their own networks of friends, relatives and work contacts that are drawn from all over the city. People in most middle-class areas are no longer constrained by geography, and are used to travelling to work or to see friends. The evidence at the Crowded House is that people are comfortable coming to explore Christianity in a home—the group is growing. The concepts of the parish and the 'local' church are no longer relevant in many communities. Indeed, it could be argued that many traditional churches engage in doublethink—placing the focus on local mission when in fact the majority of members live away from the immediate locality.

The Children's Church

Based in Deptford, south-east London, this has grown out of a congregation once linked with the Ichthus Christian Fellowship. Until recently it met every Saturday morning with up to 80 children. They have songs, games and Bible stories often led by the children themselves. This is more than just an extended children's programme or an adjunct to adult church: the adults have consciously shaped their understanding of church around Jesus' teaching about learning from children. Their Sunday and mid-week meetings also allow significant space for the full participation of children—encouraging genuine friendships to be formed between children and adults. The priority is about doing church through a child's eyes, rather than asking children to fit in around what are usually predominantly adult structures. This approach is not without its difficulties, including the demands of time and energy on a relatively small group of adults, which have led to the children's church now meeting less often. But it provides an interesting example of a differently-focused way of being church.

Pen Rhys

At the head of the Rhondda Valley, a church planted as an ecumenical initiative in a new housing development in the 1970s has a similar focus on children. It represents a very different tradition to the church in Deptford, having a formal liturgical pattern and strong institutional linkages. For many years this church struggled to make any significant headway in the isolated and dislocated community that had been forced together from all over the country to fill the new housing. When they identified education as a primary long-term need of the area and focused on supporting and complementing the work in local schools, the place of the church became more secure. Through obtaining funding for educational workers, running music lessons and choirs, developing a strong social and discipleship programme for school-age children and having school assemblies in the church on a regular basis, church has become relevant, without any attempt to entertain or 'dumb-down' the content. For example, as many as twenty children, some as young as five and many illiterate, gather to sing antiphonal Compline every Wednesday night. The current minister describes the active leadership of the church as being seventeen year olds.

Oné Respé *(Creole for 'Honour and Respect')*

It is important that we learn from situations beyond the UK. The church is being shaped in radical and exciting ways in many poorer communities around the globe. In the Dominican Republic there is considerable institutionalized racism between the Spanish-speaking, lighter-skinned Dominican population and the darker-skinned Creole-speaking population of Haitian origin. Haitians are consistently excluded from healthcare, education and economic security. In general the churches reflect the divided nature of the society. One exception to this is the community of *Oné Respé* in Santiago, who work with both sectors and bring them together to participate in shared projects of social improvement. Their approach has been to use the local radio station, which is universally listened to in the poorest areas.

One of the community leaders, an extraordinarily gifted woman from a Haitian background, broadcasts a regular programme based on Ignatian spirituality exercises. Each week she raises a different subject for meditation and reflection, such as 'How do we know God loves us?', or 'If God loves us, what is our response?' Groups then gather in the various *favellas* and talk about their individual responses to the subjects, and then consider the corporate community responses. 'How can we show love in this community?', 'What would Jesus want to change here?' These small discussion groups are regularly visited by the *Oné Respé* staff and volunteers, and they come together for larger celebrations and teaching sessions.

Given the Catholic or Voodoo backgrounds of the local people, they would not see these gatherings as church, and yet many testify to finding life and reality in their faith for the first time. Real social transformation is taking place, people are being empowered to challenge the gross injustices of their society, and the gospel is being good news for people.

The Church of the Saviour

A much more structured approach is the Church of the Saviour in Washington DC.[12] This is included not because it is new, having been active for over thirty years, but because it offers a quite different model for being church, a model which has been influential and provocative among urban church leaders in

---

12 See Elizabeth O'Connor, *Servant Leaders, Servant Structures* (Washington: The Servant Leadership School, 1991).

Britain. Here nine separate congregations have developed, each with its own ethos. They ask three questions. What is the mission in this downtown area of the city? What kind of community is needed to sustain the mission? And what set of spiritual disciplines is required to sustain that community in that mission?

They have developed congregations around a hospital for street people, a job centre, a housing association, a coffee shop and book centre, an inter-generational home caring for the elderly, to name but a few. It is possible for someone to come off the street, and to move through the ministries of the various communities: to go through detox, to find accommodation and a job and a whole new beginning in life and faith. What unites the congregations as one church is the teaching and discipleship programme that they all share in, run by the Servant Leadership School—another mission congregation. This again has a unique flavour, for they have devised a highly contextualized approach to reading Scripture and allowing the context to shape the theology. The strength of this model is the priority on mission. The mission shapes the form of the church, which seems to have a ring of gospel authenticity. This might be a good model for city-centre churches to explore.

But is it Church?
a) A Work-based Group
Christians, including directors, scientists and cleaners, meet at their place of work—a science laboratory. They pray for each other and for colleagues at work. They discuss issues of relevance to their faith and work. They occasionally share in mission activities in the work place. A participant says 'It's far more relevant and fulfilling than anything in my local church.' But it is not church—or is it?

b) The Neighbours
This is a residential community in a suburban area of Northampton. Members have neighbouring houses with their own front doors but share a huge back garden which is cultivated communally. They eat together two or three times a week and pray together every morning. Together they initiated the Daily Bread Wholefood Co-operative, which provides employment for people with mental health problems. The community was able to offer additional residential support for some of these staff members. The houses have internal connections, which make it possible for care to be shared between two households. Their priority is to live and work in ways which contribute to a fairer world. They do not call themselves church, but what are they?

c) 'Group'
'Group' has met in Oxford on Thursday nights for over five years. Drawn from over four other churches, they meet around a table in different homes, and punctuate the meal with a liturgy, songs, prayers and lots of laughter. The age

span is from eight to over sixty. During the meal current affairs are often discussed, and the relevance or otherwise of faith. Sometimes the group does Bible study together. Sometimes guests are invited; Group listens to their stories and prays for them. Members often have other contact with each other during the week and seek to care for and strengthen each others' ministries. The simple format has had a profound and sustaining impact on the lives of both regular and occasional visitors, but is it church?

d) Mill Grove

A residential home for children in East London, this has been run on a faith basis for over 100 years. It is currently home to 15 children, several single parents, two families in need and the staff and their families. They have open days and every Thursday provide lunch for local residents, who share needs and voice prayer requests. Over time they have developed, quite unconsciously, almost Benedictine patterns of life. Their director sees this as unremarkable as the Orders have developed the ideal basis for human community in terms of private and public space and patterns of work and prayer. They are so well-known and respected locally that people turn up at the door and ask how to become Christians. They talk about effortless evangelism. The director also says they are not a church. All members are encouraged to attend other local churches. But why are they not a church?

e) Urban Expression

A mission initiative of Spurgeon's College and Oasis Trust, this places teams of mainly young people in under-churched areas of East London, to work towards sharing the good news of Jesus with people around them. They do not want to use the term church until it is given to them and owned by local people. They live and work in the area, getting involved in youth clubs, football clubs and community activities. They worship in homes, and the team in Shadwell sees the most authentic form of church for that area being household-sized. They are seeking at some stage to be recognized as a Baptist Church, but is this church?

Analysing these examples shows they all reflect the key elements we identified earlier which characterized the New Testament church. They are worshipping groups who have a strong sense of community and shared life at their core. They are primarily geared around mission and service and they have, to greater and lesser extents, a fairly distinctive lifestyle. These stories provide inspiration. They offer hope. It is possible to do church differently, and in ways that appear to have a gospel impact on local communities.

4

Notes in the Margin

It has been said that the notes scribbled in the margin of any book can become the text of the next book.[13] It may be that reflection on the experiments currently taking place will provide us with the framework for a future way of being church. Here we identify some of the key challenges arising from the stories.

A Challenge to the Concept of Gathered Church

An important feature of nearly all the 'signs of hope' above is that they involve unbelievers in their community life. Lives are shared consciously with the unchurched, and the boundaries are blurred as to insiders and outsiders. The gathered church model was developed as a contrast to the parish model of the State churches which embraced all people into Christendom on the basis of geography rather than belief. Early free church leaders believed that entry into the true universal and invisible church was not by choice but was an act of God's grace. The local church was where participants in the invisible church gathered together as those called by God out of the world, to encourage each other in discipleship and in participation in God's movement of love towards the world. 'The outward church visible consists of penitent persons only and of such as believing in Christ bring forth fruits worthy of repentance.'[14] In different ways this view is also held by many beyond the free churches.

The commitment to 'believing' preceding 'belonging' was an appropriate response to the mission challenge of that era and has sustained congregational church theology since the Reformation. However, its contemporary relevance is now questioned, both by the new models and by current practice in probably the majority of churches. The present mission challenge includes a social climate in which many feel isolated from any form of community, postmodern attitudes to institutions and propositional truth, and the alienation from church that characterizes post-Christendom. Previously everyone understood what church was about and most felt they belonged to a greater or lesser extent. This is no longer true, and if the gospel is to make sense it seems essential that unbelievers are embraced within the Christian community and can witness the life-transforming practice of the gospel.

Many churches are responding, instinctively or deliberately, by adopting a philosophy of 'belonging' preceding 'believing.' So has the concept of 'gathered

---

13 On marginal hermeneutics, see Terry Veling, *Living in the Margins—Intentional Community and the Art of Interpretation* (New York: Crossroad Herder, 1996).
14 Quoted in A C Underwood, *A History of the English Baptists* (London: Carey Kingsgate Press, 1947) p 41, and taken from *The Works of John Smyth Vol 2*, p 81.

church' any contemporary currency? Is the concept of a 'gathering church' more helpful? Is a dynamic model for people on a journey more liberating than a static model that separates believers and unbelievers? Is a community with a 'bonded centre' more appropriate than either an all-encompassing parish model or a church with fixed boundaries?

A Challenge to Denominationalism and Ecumenism

Concern for Christian unity has been a major thrust during the past century. The impact of the ecumenical movement, Vatican II and many other expressions of this concern have been profound. But experiments with new ways of being church result in increasing diversity. Do new forms of church threaten the movement towards Christian unity?

The proliferation of experiments is extending the post-denominational trend which has been apparent for several years. Old tribal labels (Anglican, Baptist, House Church, Methodist, Pentecostal) and loyalties which once hindered ecumenical progress seem increasingly irrelevant. Christians moving home generally choose a new church not by its label, but for such factors as its style of worship, quality of teaching, sense of community, concern for justice, commitment to mission. Weaker denominational ties might be considered advantageous in working towards unity but, in a postmodern context, institutions, hierarchies, bureaucratic structures and grand schemes are all suspect. Grass-roots action, small groups and networking are preferred ways of relating and operating.

Will we need to find new ways of working with this tension, celebrating diversity more wholeheartedly and pursuing a messier form of unity, which goes beyond the currently accepted denominational bodies and ecumenical processes? Will the ecumenism of the future be local rather than national, grass-roots rather than structural, rooted in mission partnership rather than doctrinal agreement?

A Challenge to Ways of Celebrating Communion

The centrality of sharing a meal together is critical in many of the new models of church. It also seems very significant in the development of any community life within a church. The success of the *Alpha* courses, some would argue for example, has much to do with the central feature of the shared meal. In some expressions of church this has developed an acknowledged liturgical significance—it is that community's expression of Communion. In others, they would still take part in the more formal celebration of the Lord's Supper within their tradition, but in real terms view the community meal-times as the high points of genuine 'communion' with God and with the gathered fellowship.

Participants in some of the new ways of being church would argue that the meal Jesus shared with his disciples, and the pattern that developed in the first few centuries of Christian life, was very much a normal supper shared with friends and that the symbolic practices, that have developed through Christendom, have been a distortion. This development is now challenged in the context of smaller, more intimate expressions of Christian community. What are the gains and losses of celebrating communion in a more informal and domestic setting?

A Challenge to Leadership

It is significant that fewer than half the initiatives above are clergy-led. Is this because the clergy have a vested interest in keeping in place the power structures of traditional churches? Smaller forms of church rely more on shared leadership, participation and consensual government. They may not require full-time leadership. This presents an implicit challenge to the relevance of ordination and paid ministry. However, the long-term implications for theological literacy within the Christian community could be worrying. Many colleges are already moving towards more flexible schemes of training for different kinds of non-ordained ministry. Will new structures need to emerge to ensure appropriate and on-going training?

A Challenge to the Focus of Church life

In several of the models, children are very central to the way of being church, and actually making church accessible to children has changed the dynamic of church life. This begs questions about taking Jesus seriously when he talks about making the least the greatest. If children, and being like children, are in some way decisive in understanding and entering the kingdom of God, then surely forms of church need to build on this? Children are perhaps only one example. Jesus also pointed to other vulnerable groups and those on the outside of the mainstream. What does church begin to look like when we put those on the margins into the centre?

The challenge posed is whether a community submits its own preferences and needs to meet those of the marginalized group, and what impact and witness might this have. Usually the needs of the most powerful and educated dominate a community. As those committed to overthrowing domination systems, would not a genuinely gospel church affirm those of least importance or significance?

A Challenge to Our Language

Many of the examples described above did not set out to become church at all and thus were unconstrained by the expectations attached to the word 'church.' This seems to free groups to develop more imaginative schemes, which have greater relevance to the context in which they are set. Perhaps we should consider a moratorium on the word 'church,' because it is vested with too many preconceptions and too much baggage. It carries many connotations of Christendom that hinder creativity and radical action and does nothing to encourage those outside the church to explore faith in such an institution. Might it be better that we learn to live as Christian community, consciously doing kingdom work, and allow others to name us, once we have earned the right to be identified as the followers of the Way?

A Challenge to Our Priorities

Several of the stories reflect a process of church following mission activity, almost as an accident. Perhaps the traditional priority of viewing church as a worshipping (worship service based) community first and foremost is a hindrance to creative responses to a changing society.

Robert Warren's simple diagram encapsulates something important about the essential nature of church.[15] It requires these three elements, of worship, community and mission and only when these three are equally present and fully informing each other does Christian spirituality find true expression.

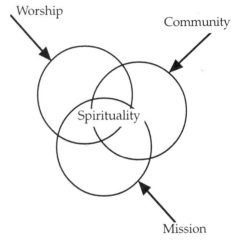

Worship

Community

Spirituality

Mission

What this diagram also expresses is the ways *into* being church. Traditionally the primary way in was through worship—one established a worship centre, and then moved towards developing these other two elements as and when the time was right.

Much recent church planting has followed this model. A group has been transplanted into an area and begun to worship, and gradually invited others to join them. We heard recently about a church plant that is struggling. They have been worshipping on an estate for nearly ten years, but it transpires that that is all they do—they do not live locally—they come from all over so their community life is underdeveloped and they have no clear sense of mission. Is it surprising that they are struggling to be church? Too much church planting has been limited by the notion that church is first and foremost about establishing a worshipping group, and many church plants have merely become small replicas of mother churches.

What people are beginning to discover is that one can actually enter church

---

15 Robert Warren, *Being Human, Being Church* (London: Marshall Pickering, 1995)—diagram adapted slightly.

from any of these points. A community committing itself to one another and to seeking God's will together, can become church. A group coming together to do a specific mission task can become church. They can equally get stuck if they do not grow into developing the other circles—because a whole and integrated Christian spirituality requires these three elements in tension.

A Challenge to the Christendom Mentality

Although we are moving steadily into a post-Christendom environment, where the church is increasingly marginal and Christianity is but one of many options in a pluralistic society, the Christendom mindset remains strong within many churches. Reflexes and reactions, as well as structures and expectations, suggest that we have not yet really come to terms with the loss of ecclesiastical power, status, wealth and social centrality. It is unlikely that the privileges churches enjoyed under Christendom will be sustained indefinitely, and many would argue that disestablishment may free the church to respond more radically to the challenges of contemporary society. This has import not only for the established church, but also for many free churches which are often even more committed to the Christendom model of church life.

A vital task as we enter the third millennium is to discover new ways of being church that operate from the margins, do not require as much institutional support, are less grandiose and expensive to maintain, abandon an inappropriate moral majority stance in favour of a prophetic vocation, and embody the missionary ethos appropriate in post-Christendom.

The theological challenges to our ecclesiology represented by the stories we have told are challenges that will face increasing numbers of churches over the coming years. These stories do not provide us with all the answers or even all point us in the same direction, but they may help us recognize some of the important questions. However, changing the shape of the church is risky. There may be losses as well as gains. We will explore some of these in the final chapter.

5

Gains and Losses

The new models of church pose many questions. Here we examine just a few of the tensions inherent in the stories.

Presence or Hiddenness

Most of our examples have been fairly visible, but some of them and many cell churches, alternative worship networks and post-evangelical-type groups are not visible or accessible to the public. What does this mean for evangelism and social action? We recognize that early churches grew at a phenomenal rate through the fascination they exerted without buildings or public meetings. But their members lived in much smaller and closer-knit communities. How does this translate into anonymous urban and suburban twenty-first century communities? The strategy of Crowded House makes sense in a highly mobile, middle-class community and may show us a way forward in such areas. Here, a building is considered an anathema, loading church life with false expectations and unhelpful baggage.

Yet a building continually exerts pressure on a church to be locally relevant, to think about serving the neighbourhood around it, because it occupies social space. It flags up the word 'mission' even if the congregation ignores it. A hidden church can easily lose its outward focus and its call to subvert and serve society. A hidden church is also vulnerable if ever it wants funding for a social project. Local Authorities and Trusts are very wary of sects. Pen Rhys and Burngreave have attracted massive funding because they are backed by several major denominations. Less recognizable groups stand to lose opportunities for significant social transformation, unless strong alliances and partnerships can be constructed. How important is this?

Engaged and Distinctive

Holy Joe's, Epicentre, Grace and *London Underground* are examples of alternative worship groups which could loosely be described as post-evangelical. This term was popularised by Dave Tomlinson,[16] as he explained his growing distaste for what he identified as oppressive forms of church life exemplified within much of the House Church movement. A key aspect of these alternatives is a rejection of the Christian sub-culture, which is deemed sub-standard. The aim of many of these groups is to use music and the arts from the contemporary cul-

---

16 Tomlinson, *The Post-Evangelical*. For examples of other such groups, and reflection on these, see Paul Roberts, *Alternative Worship in the Church of England* (Cambridge: Grove Books, 1999).

ture, rather than Christianised versions, and to create an experience that is not embarrassing nor alien to their non-Christian friends. However, the attempt to engage with contemporary culture can result in a wholesale accommodation to the prevailing sub-culture—especially the culture of young professionals or youth. Escape from the ghetto and engagement with some dimensions of the surrounding culture are liberating to many participants, but exploring Christian distinctives in lifestyle and community do not appear to be on the agenda.

A contrasting approach is that of writers such as Stanley Hauerwas[17] and Rodney Clapp.[18] They are calling the Christian community to be radically different in every area of life—to model an alternative society which shows that it is possible to live, for example, simply *and* joyfully, that it is possible to live in a way that releases significant resources to be re-distributed to the developing world. No amount of shouting about increasing overseas aid is going to make a real difference until a significant proportion of the voting population is prepared to live in a way that enables it to happen. Yet we have very few examples of this working out in practice. Some intentional communities, such as the Jesus Fellowship and the Bruderhof, do live distinctively but to many they appear alienating. Is there a third way emerging in some of the smaller community-based churches? Do they show us ways to be both engaged and distinctive?

Immanence and Transcendence

Our culture at present is deeply interested in the transcendent. People are responding to ritual and symbolism in new ways—witness the candles and flowers for Princess Diana, or at the scene of accidents. The growth of the Orthodox Church in Britain may be partially explained by this, as may conversions to Anglo-Catholicism. People are still wanting to mark rites of passage these days—and not just the traditional rites of christenings, weddings and funerals. Ministers are often asked to help people mark wedding anniversaries, divorces, new jobs, moving house and other important events.

Consequently it is ironic that, just when ritual is again in vogue, many churches are moving away from traditional and more sacramental expressions of church life. Many new ways of being church use domestic settings and informal styles of worship and relating. They are strong on immanence, seeking to discern the signs of God at work in their lives, relationships and neighbourhoods. But it is hard to create a transcendent experience around your kitchen table. Similarly, the potential 'disappearance' of ordained ministers may make responding to felt needs beyond the church more difficult. Are there ways in which ritual and symbolism can be reclaimed and adapted for such settings?

17 Stanley Hauerwas and William Willimon, *Resident Aliens: Life in the Christian Colony* (Nashville, TN: Abingdon Press, 1989).
18 Rodney Clapp, *A Peculiar People: the Church as Culture in a Post-Christian Society* (Downers Grove, Ill: IVP, 1996).

Planting or Renewal

We have limited time and energy, so where do we invest this—in working for renewal within existing forms of church, or in planting new forms of church? We have included stories of both. There are passionate advocates of each approach, who dismiss the alternative as counter-productive. A major debate within the Charismatic Movement in the 1970s and early 1980s revolved around the terms 'stay in' or 'come out,' 'renewal' or 'restoration.' This has been a perennial issue throughout church history, at least since the Montanist movement of the second century.

Is it possible that both kinds of initiatives are needed? That God calls individuals and communities to different tasks? That new forms of church can draw on the experience of more established forms and that the institutions can learn from the experiments of the pioneers, so that together we can discern what the Spirit might be saying? That this symbiosis could result in synergy and advances in mission?

Small or Large

Mark Greene, in a recent review of Tom Sine's *Mustard Seed versus McWorld*,[19] criticizes Sine's 'seeds of hope' for all being too small and marginal. The same criticism would apply to all the stories we have told. Greene wants more far-reaching examples of change and transformation, which would have greater impact on our society. This begs questions about how God's kingdom comes in our society. Can we be content with mustard seed changes, or do we need large and powerful churches that have wider significance and command respect? Many still value the privileges accorded to the church during the Christendom era and are loathe to give these up. Relinquishing power and status is hard, but what is the gospel way of being church? Do we want to be key players in civic society by virtue of our office or our numerical strength, rather than through the quality of our lives and communities?

Independence and Accountability

At present most emerging forms are connected to the wider institutional church, but will this remain so as time moves on and if the institutions become weaker? If distinctive new ways of being church develop, will they continue to value their institutional links, and will the institutions want to be associated with them? Small, informal groupings are great in the short term, but they raise longer-term questions. Another significant issue is accountability and participation in the wider disciplines of the church. Many know the story of the Nine O'Clock Service in Sheffield, and there are other sorry tales of groups that have failed to be accountable.

19 *Baptist Times*, 22nd July 1999, p 12.

Threatened also are the possibilities of political co-ordination. Campaigns such as Jubilee 2000 need the co-ordinating power of the institutional churches. How can we be subversive politically if we have no national structures? What will this do to organizations like Christian Aid—can hidden groups spearhead the collection for an area, or will it lose credibility? Can such organizations become flexible enough to work with less formal structures?

Permanence or Transience

The prevailing trend has been that churches are established to last indefinitely and to be a permanent sign of the presence of God in an area. However, aiming for such permanence may not always be appropriate. Some new forms of church are tentative and experimental. Mission-based churches may only be established for as long as the mission exists. A mobile population may come together as community for a certain time and then disperse. There is a tension here in the time taken for genuine community to form, as there are many examples of how churches struggled until a few key people committed themselves to stay for a minimum of twenty years. This gave confidence and a stability that enabled life to grow.

Readiness to close down institutions once they have accomplished their task is not often apparent (the closure of the Fountain Trust was an impressive exception), but ageing institutions may become a hindrance to effective mission. How important is it to the witness of a Christian community to stay in a local area and remain committed to people? In some rural and inner-city areas this would seem to be very important, but might it be less so in those more middle-class areas which tend to be more mobile anyway?

Inner City and Suburban

We recognize that most examples of new ways of being church are emerging in the inner city and on urban estates, where poverty issues are dominant. It could be argued that it is relatively easy to develop new ways in situations where people have very little to lose. It is also relatively simple for the church to develop relevant social ministries. However, the majority of our churches are in more comfortable areas where needs are more hidden and lives are extraordinarily busy. As yet, there are very few examples of doing things very differently in suburbia. Perhaps the presence of some very large thriving churches seduces us into thinking that the old ways are still relevant. Unfortunately, however, the resources absorbed by some of the mega-churches just cannot be matched in all suburban churches, and the pale reflections, in terms of the quality of worship and ambience, do not attract or hold people.

Box Hill Baptist Church was a reasonably 'successful' middle-class church in Melbourne, Australia. Its members recognized that, despite its size and wide range of activities, it was not actually touching the people in the immediate neighbourhood of the church. They took the brave step of saying that, since the church existed for mission, they must stop all that they were doing in order to get the mission right. They closed down for nine months. During this time, every church member undertook to join a local club or group such as the darts team in a pub, an art class, a keep-fit group, a political party. Their only church activity was a meeting every Wednesday for the first six months to look at the biblical, sociological and psychological nature of church in the light of what they were learning about the local community from the clubs and societies they had joined. They then took the next three months to work out a new way of being church in the light of all they had discovered. Within the first year of their new incarnation they had an influx of local people.

Do authentic new ways of being church always require this kind of risk, of letting go, and of deep commitment to listening to God and to those outside the church? Can church be different and life-changing in *all* sectors of society if the people of God genuinely want it to be so?

Watching the Margins

Culturally we are led by success. Industry, commerce and entertainment are dominated by initiatives that have grown and prospered, and very often the Christian community is seduced along the same path. We are dazzled by the mega-churches and suburban success stories. The wealthy, large and prosperous churches command respect. God, however, so often seems to work on the margins, in unlikely places, in powerless communities. Witness the extraordinary bathos of the following passage from Luke's gospel:

> 'In the fifteenth year of the reign of Tiberias Caesar—when Pontius Pilate was governor of Judea, Herod tetrarch of Galilee, his brother Philip tetrarch of Iturea and Traconitis, and Lysanias tetrarch of Abilene—during the high priesthood of Annas and Caiaphas, the word of God came to *John, son of Zechariah in the desert.*'
>
> (Luke 3.1–2)

It is our contention that we should watch the margins and discover the activity of God in the inner-city, on the housing estates, in the prisons, amongst refugee groups. Already we can feel the influence of historical movements that were never part of Christendom, as increasing numbers in search of alternative ways of being church explore Celtic spirituality and Anabaptist radical discipleship. It is these movements that were marginalized by the prevailing powers of their time that seem to offer alternative perspectives for a post-Christendom society. Similarly, we may need to look less to North America and more to the Two-Thirds world for partners, who have already moved out from under colonial patterns, and who can help us understand our own culture and discover more fitting patterns for our society.

The emphasis in the coming years must be on contextual missiology and ecclesiology, which involves careful listening to those beyond the church walls, and to those prophetic voices on the margins of church life.

Above all, regardless of the shape of new forms of church, we need to refocus on centring the life of the Christian community on Christ. Jesus was born in poverty and obscurity, and spent much of his life challenging the social pressures to use existing power structures. His way challenges the focus of our attention. It is our conviction that we live in a society that is heartily sick of Christianity and of the institutional church but that has yet to encounter the radical Jesus. New ways of being church need also to be new ways of telling the story of Jesus and helping people to encounter him. And it may be the story of Jesus, rather than doctrinal beliefs about Jesus, that will prove to be our most potent evangelistic resource. Walter Wink suggests: 'In the spiritual renaissance that I believe is coming to birth, it will not be the message of Paul that this time galvanizes hearts, as in the Reformation and the Wesleyan revival, but the human figure of Jesus.'[20] It may be that the teaching, relationships, values and character of the Jesus of the gospels will be the crucial points of contact with contemporary culture. What way of being church will reveal this Jesus to our society? It would be tragic if we only explored new ways of being church and failed to discover new ways of telling and living the story of Jesus.

For Further Reading

In addition to books featured in the footnotes, we suggest:

Dave Andrews, *Christi-anarchy—discovering a radical spirituality of compassion* (Tring: Lion, 1999)
Mary Beasley, *Mission on the Margins* (Cambridge: Lutterworth Press, 1997)
Gene Edwards, *How to Meet* (Beaumont: Message Ministry, 1993)
Stuart Murray, *Church Planting—Laying Foundations* (Carlisle: Paternoster, 1998)
Meic Pearse and Chris Matthews, *We must stop meeting like this* (Eastbourne: Kingsway, 1999)
Mike Riddell, *Threshold of the Future* (London: SPCK, 1998)

We invite readers to join with us in the process of gathering further hopeful stories and writing more notes in the margin. If you know of any initiatives which interest or stimulate you, then please do let us know of them, by writing to us at: Spurgeon's College, 189 South Norwood Hill, London SE25 6DJ.

---

20 Walter Wink, *Engaging the Powers* (Minneapolis: Fortress Press, 1992) p 263.